A Myriad Of Emotions

A Myriad Of Emotions

ISBN (kdp): 9798740887494
ISBN (print copy): 978-1-955762-02-1
ISBN (ebook copy): 978-1-955762-05-2

Front cover image by Nicki Snyder.

Published by TheShyWriter
www.theshywriter.org

I'd like to dedicate this book to my poetry group.

Your encouragement and camaraderie inspires me to continue writing and sharing.

Thank-you.

Other books by Nicki Snyder:

The Circus Elephant

Howie

No Hope Beyond This Point

#cloudart

Table of Contents

Introduction:

Hi. Thank you for purchasing this book, or for borrowing it from a friend or a library. Either way, I like that you made this your reading choice.

Inside are poems (and a few very short stories at the end) that cover a wide range of emotions; some positive, some negative, but none that are too heavy.

And just one thing before you delve in, I thought I'd tell you about the way the book is set up, as it might be slightly different from other poetry books you've read.

As I was formatting, I thought about where my eyes tend to gravitate when I turn a page. Perhaps it's because I'm right-handed, but I look at the right page first, then the left, and so I chose to start all of the poems on the right side.

On the left side you'll find something about the poem; a description, a how-to, a story, a picture I took, or a drawing I did. (Though sometimes the drawings are on the right.)

That's it. Thank you again for picking up this book. I hope you find something that speaks to you.

annotation:

The Grind is a local coffee
shop in my area where I occasionally meet up
with fellow poets to share poetry.

The Grind

Ground to dust and blown away
Yet here we are, we sit and stay

Gathered up with frothy mirth
The fireplace with heat gives birth

To warmth and laughter, ideas spill
We share our words and help to fill

This space of friends and welcome, too
We stir together to say what's new

annotation:

When I first started going to my local poetry meetings, I was a bit intimidated by the level everyone was at, so I decided to bring something more complex.
I did some research and tried my hand at writing a Paradelle, however, it wasn't really in my voice. I found that I liked the poem better without the repeating lines.

The rules are:

4 stanzas, each 6 lines long.

The 1st 3 stanzas:

The first line is original. Repeat it for the second line.
The third line is original. Repeat it for the fourth line.
Lines 5 and 6 are made up of all the words used in lines 1 and 3, but are rearranged to make something new. (You can only use each word once.)

The 4th stanza has no repeating lines, and is made up solely of the original words you wrote in the above stanzas, but rearranged.

Here is my condensed version:

A Paradelle Poem

What wonders behold my eyes?

To take in all that surrounds me

Technology shows us so much

Do we glance up to see more?

Beauty in nature, in others too

How much we miss and do not appreciate

Do not miss too much in nature,

And how we appreciate beauty in others

Take that in; technology and beauty, too

More wonders we see in others' eyes

Do not miss what surrounds us

Glance up – so much to behold.

My, how much we do!

Nature shows me to appreciate in all

annotation:

Here is another paradelle poem minus the repeating lines.
This one was inspired by a neighbor who always parked in
front of my house instead of hers.

Annoyed

The whole street is empty
One lone car, parked. **Not mine**
The empty street is mine
Not one whole, lone, parked car

Is there nowhere else to go?
Oh, but there is. **Not here**
To go there is not here
There is nowhere else. But, oh?

Where is your house? This one is mine
Move your car. Be gone please
This house, where your car is, is mine
Please move your one. **Be gone**

Your lone car is here, but mine is there
Oh, please be gone whole car
Is there nowhere not parked?
Is this one not mine?
Where else is the street empty?
One move. **GO TO YOUR HOUSE**

annotation:

I found a lot of inspiration for poetry while I was a
sophomore in college.

Early Morning Class

The alarm clock sounds relentlessly.
He struggles out of bed.
Eyelids heavy; a pillow so soft.
A blanket too warm; ice cold air.

He splashes water on his face in the bathroom.
Relief is sought, but is only temporarily offered.

Clothes thrown on.
Teeth and hair brushed.
Backpack flung over shoulder.

Heading out the door.
A giant yawn escapes his mouth.
The bed beckons from the other room.

School is loudly calling.
Sleep will have to wait.

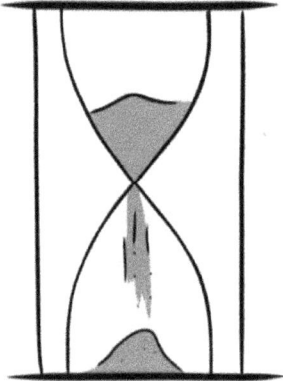

Fleeting Freedom

They sat in the room, the clock ticking away
Waiting for it to strike the hour
And let them leave

The day was nice
The sun was out for once
But most had work after classes
Of which, there were still many left to go

They wanted to be reminded of their youth
To enjoy the gorgeous day outside
How depressing it felt

To be cooped up
Stuck in buildings all day long
With the harsh florescent lights boring down

They needed a break from responsibility
They needed freedom

annotation:

In the course of one day, I managed to mishear my daughter twice. The first time was when she was helping me find masculine or "dudely" honorifics. (The 1st line.)

The second time she was making pasta for dinner and tried to tell me the water was starchy. (Hence the 2nd line.)

Either way, I thought the misheard words worked together in a poem. They made me think of a man on a paddle board, taking his time, as he travels over both the choppy and calm waters of life.

Misheard

Dudely on a rivicks
in the sturgy waters
traversing down the rapids
to only-god-knows where

annotation:

I'm so often lost in daydreams or worries that feeling disconnected is a common-enough issue for me.

Not Here

I often feel like I'm not here.
I don't know where I am or where I go.

My thoughts tend to drift away
as my eyes get hazy and glaze over.

I feel like I could be anywhere
or nowhere all at once.

I try to stay focused
with my feet firmly planted on the ground,
but there I go, wondering away again.

I wish I could tell you where I go,
but it seems a mystery, even to me.

All I can say is: I'm not here.

annotation:

A smaller subset of my poetry group started meeting
online every Wednesday.

Wednesdays

Content and calm
Happy and harmonious

Gathering with like minds
Seeing familiar faces

Hearing voices belonging to friends

Peace I don't find during the days
I find now in the evenings

Gathered round my screen
Sharing time with poets

Jokes, smiles, and laughter
Concerns are shared

Worried times forgotten
Alleviated in the moment

Thoughts

The feelings I have
Is love for everything live.
How content I am.

annotation:

There was an internet rumor going around saying the moon and stars would make a smiley face in the sky. It wasn't true, but it was a nice thought.

4/29/20

May Fifteen, Twenty
Michelle said to watch the sky
Moon, planets will smile

annotation:

Who wasn't affected in some way by the coronavirus shutdown?

Here are three poems expressing how I felt at the beginning of the crisis, during our "safer at home" order, and when my state started opening back up.

Quarantine

Sadly sitting
Softly still

Stressed and strained
Somberly sullen

Waiting. Watching
Wild, wide eyes

Wanting wisdom
Wistful – but waning

When will we go back to normal?

Work, home, sleep, repeat
Work, home, sleep, repeat

I drag myself out of bed
Stare at my phone
While I brush the hair on my head

I go to work, she goes to school
We both carry on
We have a lot to do

I watch the news
The whispers abound
'bout a virus that is going around

We get up the next day
And it all repeats
Work, home, sleep
Work, home, sleep

Little changes
But the news, it swells
We do our routines
And I dwell and dwell

But we carry on as we always do
Changing little about our attitude

Til one day – all of it cracks
The dam, it breaks
Now we see what we've lacked

Shutdowns begin
And we're stuck inside
Our routine is broken
Our fear is high

Our pattern, it changes
Yet still repeats
To something else
A newer beat

Home, sleep
Home, sleep

And now we struggle to make amends
To rectify and define our sins
To find the blame but heal too
For together we must learn to do
Something we had not done before
Find a new way, open a door

Look out for ourselves
And our neighbors too
We must find a new avenue

We can't cling to the idea of our old routines
Change has come and it might remain

Forced to explore ways to stay safe
A new mantra chanted, begrudgingly embraced

Home, home, home, home

But we all are antsy and unsure
Stuck inside, angry and bored
Wondering what comes next, if we'll survive
Demanding to know when we can go outside

We look to our leaders, our friends as well
Needing to have anxiety quelled
Pondering aloud our biggest fear
Hoping that the answer is near

But have we changed, and is it enough?
Did we make a large enough fuss?

For if we emerge and forget what we've learned
The disease will come back and when it returns
Lockdowns will ensue
With panic anew

And we'll be left asking again
When will we go back to normal?

Second Round

Isolated
An animal in a cage

I can see people
but communication is hard

Gone is the ease
The connection is fading

Masks, shields
and closed doors now rule

As a social creature
I want to rally against this!

Angst and fear rise up
demanding attention

Misery and loneliness
hang in the air; suffocating

I'm being dramatic
I am aware

But wisdom and sanity prevail
Stay safe. Keep others safe

This shall pass
and we *will* connect again

annotation:

I wanted to try something different for a writing prompt my local group suggested. I thought I'd try and challenge myself, so I wrote a poem in the style of Poe's "The Raven".

A Smile Upon Her Face

I see a smile upon her face, it warms my heart to view her grace

That she took the time to grin like that, rushing about in a flurry

The current smile I see her wear, is something I helped to put there

Into her car, she leaves with care. Then, takes off in a hurry

I get to work not far behind. I see her now. The love I've pined

I set my stuff upon my desk. She calls, "Good Morning, Murray"

I know her name, and she knows mine. We've been neighbors for quite some time

Her name is Anne and she's divine. A soft heart full of worry

What can I do to ease her strain? This thought is a common refrain

Wanting to help. Showing I care. I've made this my sworn duty

Her charm, her wit, her attitude; I don't spout a mere platitude

Everything about Anne exudes a kindness, peace and beauty

My heart alights. I meet her eyes. But hide my feelings behind lies

We've worked together for several years, life bringing us closer

I've tried to tell her; to confess, but every time I make a mess

With hidden love, I shrink her stress, maintaining my composure

One day I trip, and words spill out. Anne hears each sound, I have no doubt

I reach out to snatch them back. A futile effort; zilch to grab

The secret's out, and now she knows. I want to crawl into a hole

I brace myself. Prepare my soul. Knowing her rebuff will stab

But nothing comes. I squint my eyes, and see a grin to my surprise

She takes in a breath and tells me this, "Murray, your heart is kind.

I have something I must confess. I'm hurt to see you in distress

I love you more, you know, not less. Far too long, we've both been blind"

I straighten up, courageous now. I admit I've helped her and how

Trash forgotten in morning haste, is moved by me to the curb

Mail piled up on the building floor, I set those boxes at her door

Anne's favorite candy from the store, slyly left to not disturb

"I have witnessed these things you hide. Buried deeply beneath your pride

You make me happy," Anne delights. "Though I have more to declare.

I too have done some little things in hope to make your spirit sing

I fixed your jacket tear with string, the favored one you like to wear

You left it sitting on your chair, I stole it. Sorry. To repair

Another thing I'd like to divulge is why I'm late most days

The morning paper that you find, I sneak there and leave it behind

The paperboy is not inclined to place it where it should lay"

We share a laugh, a kiss, a hug. Warmth spreads thru us, our arms so snug

And after our secrets are laid bare, I tell her what I think:

You go through life with such finesse, and to this question please say yes

To be with you would be a bless. Would you like to get a drink?

Growing Up

Growing up. A goal everyone seeks to obtain.

As a young child, you wear your parent's clothes
and mimic them.
You think, "Oh, it's a wonderful thing to be an adult."

As a teen, you try to be your own person;
to act grown-up.
You think, "I am not a child. I can act like an adult."

As a young adult, you spread your wings
and begin to fly.
You think, "I can finally do what I want. I'm an adult."

As you age, you begin to realize that growing up
is a pain more often than not.
Now you think, "How I wish I was young again."

annotation:

Someone I follow on Twitter put up a beautiful poem on Valentine's Day. It was really quite eloquent.

I thought it only fitting to return his poem with one of my own, so this is what I posted:

A small poem

On this day of San Valentin
Remember to be kind, and not to be mean

Give everyone a smile with not an ounce of strife
Let them feel cherished for at least one day of life

And maybe, perhaps, when tomorrow is new
You'll carry this forward to every day, too

annotation:

Who hasn't felt that their thoughts and ambitions were greater than their desire to accomplish the tasks they've set for themselves?

<u>Bursting at the seams</u>

Too Many Tasks
Too Many Goals
stretching myself into spaghetti

So Many Plans
So Many Thoughts
like cotton erupting from a pillow

How to accomplish all that I want?

My ambition runs circles around my motivation

annotation:

A friend, and fellow poet, wrote a haiku called "Day in A-minor". It brought back my years in band, and I returned his poem with a musical haiku and dodoitsu of my own.

Rules:

Haiku: 3 lines of 5, 7, 5 syllables, usually about nature

Dodoitsu: 4 lines of 7, 7, 7, 5 syllables, usually about love or work with a funny twist at the end

Counter Measure

b-sharp, be clever
rise up the scale, throw off doubt
it's harmonious

Same Bar

conversations rise and fall
yet I stay right here with you
on this bar, it's just we two
hang out here often?

annotation:

I find that it gets my creative juices flowing if I try different poetry styles. This is a Villanelle.

"Do not go gentle into that good night" is a famous example.

The setup is 4+ three-lined stanzas, followed by 1 four-lined stanza. Each stanza has an ABA rhyme scheme, with lines that repeat throughout the poem.
See below:

ABA
AB,repeat 1st line
AB,repeat 3rd line
AB,repeat 1st line
AB, repeat 3rd line
AB,repeat 1st line, repeat 3rd line

First Attempt

Life has really got me stressed
A head not screwed on right
My behavior might need to be addressed

I know that I can attest
My thoughts drift off like a kite
Life has really got me stressed

Today I didn't get dressed
At least not until it was night
My behavior might need to be addressed

My mop of hair not brushed is a nest
A wonderful place for birds to alight
Life has really got me stressed

I woke up chipper, but then regressed
So back to bed. I fought a good fight
My behavior might need to be addressed

I started the day with real zest
And tried with all my might
But... Life has really got me stressed
My behavior might need to be addressed

annotation:

While at work, I listened to the sound of trees being cut down and ground up. This always makes me sad, even if their removal is justified.

Sounds of Progress

Grinding down trees
Never putting them back

Tearing up landscapes
Laying down tracks

Where does nature go
When we've filled her all in?

What do we eat and breathe
When we've tarmacked our sin?

Bitter Days

It started out all fluffy white
    falling from the sky
But soon it turned against us all
    unloading on the land
The sky turned dark, the ground was slick
    everything was covered

Livid, fuming people - continuing to drive
    had curses on their lips
While wiper blades tried hard to clean
    cars slid about in traffic

For months on end the anger stayed
    grouchiness it lingered
'Til hearts they melted with the snow
    and sun reclaimed the sky

People grinned; their tempers calmed
    donning shorts and tees
Ignoring facts that in a few short months
    the cycle would repeat

When lessons lost and forgotten
    only to relearn
As snow does gather in the sky
    releasing once again

annotation:

My friend shared a story, which showed me that even if you lose a companion, love endures. I find that very comforting.

Enduring Love:

rose petals in a jar

their scent wafts to me

when I open it

I'm reminded of you.

annotation:

This untitled poem is called a cherita. It's Malaysian for "story" or "tale". It is not supposed to be titled, from what I read, and can be written by 1-3 people.

The poem consists of a 1-line stanza, a 2-line stanza, and a 3-line stanza in that order.

(untitled)

I walked tall down the road.

My knee clicked
with each step.

I annoyed myself
but didn't stop
until the path was done.

annotation:

I love staring into space, but the idea of actually being out there scares me.
I'd make a very bad companion for the Doctor.

Night Sky

The vastness of space
scares her so.

But the wonder of the stars
holds her in their throes.

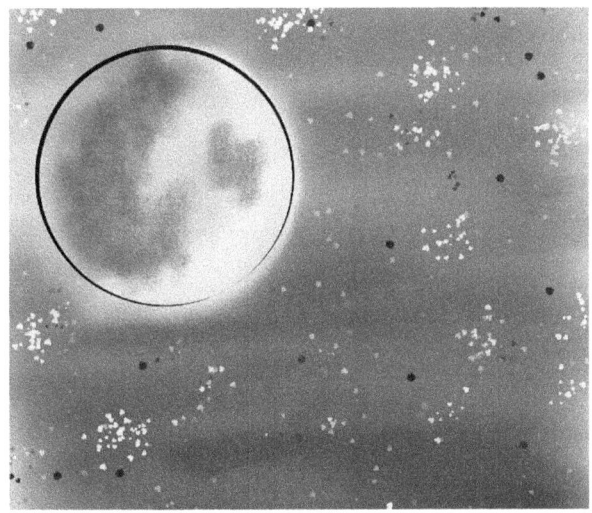

annotation:

I submitted these 4 "stories" to a publication that only asks
for original-style tweets of 140 characters.
They weren't accepted, but I thought that, when combined,
they made a nice poem.

140 Characters At A Time

What does one hundred and forty characters look like?
A deep thought? Or a wisp of an idea?
Can I pour my heart out or will I run out of roo

I'll try again to make my thoughts fit in this narrow space.
I'll think quick and short. I'll type in txt spk to save room.
It can be done.

I managed to have a left over character but I can't carry it over.
It floats there, unused. It's mine. I want it.
I could say so much there.

Why limit ourselves physically and psychologically?
Expand; explore; spread out.
Push past the limitations, or embrace them.
Make them more.

annotation:

This is a pantoum poem; a Malaysian style from the 15th century, which was later adapted by the French.

The scheme is 4 lined stanzas with a repeating pattern:

Line 1	Line 2	Line 5	Line 7
Line 2	Line 5	Line 7	Line 3
Line 3	Line 4	Line 6	Line 8
Line 4	Line 6	Line 8	Line 1

You can repeat the middle pattern for as long as you want. It's my understanding that the repetition is used to make the poem sound like a chant.

Twisting Back

Trapped; walking down the hall
Familiar faces, familiar steps
Repeating, retreating, returning
It's all the same; there is no escape

Familiar faces, familiar steps
A loop never-ending; frightening
It's all the same; there is no escape
A horrific nightmare of sameness

A loop never-ending; frightening
See the end? Run!
A horrific nightmare of sameness
You trip and hit the mirage

See the end? Run!
It shimmers and beckons
You trip and hit the mirage
A dead-end until it starts over

It shimmers and beckons
Repeating, retreating, returning
A dead-end until it starts over
Trapped; walking down the hall

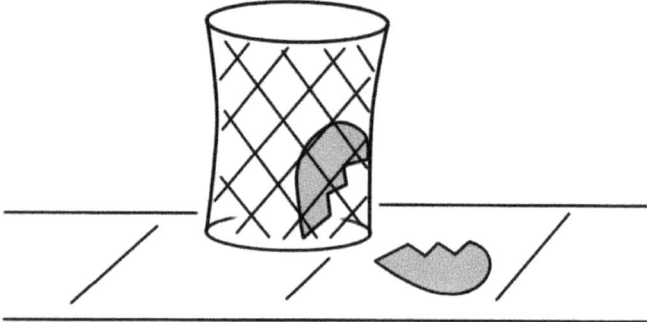

FAIRY TALE

A sweetness like wine,

a love that's divine,

held true every word.

The truth tho, it hurts.

A dream we must wake

and with it we know

that nothing is real.

Your love, it is fake.

annotation:

A fellow writer described this poem as "spilling stress onto paper" and I agree.

I'm one to hold things in, so writing my feelings down is cathartic even if I don't say why I feel strained.

Emoting

Mess
Stress
Confess

I feel I'm causing it myself

Calm
Balm
Qualm

No, it is not all internal

Strain
Refrain
Contain

I push the tension down inside

Pout
Doubt
Shout

I need the words out to move on

Alight
Write
Plight

annotation:

This is a tanka poem, which is written like a haiku but with two extra lines that are 7 syllables each.

Happiness

Where can I find it?
Does he have it? Does she? Them?
What makes me happy?
A smile forms as I ponder
Family, friends, writing – found it

Writing

Yearning for words
Time spent typing

Thoughts come too fast
Thoughts come too slow

Did I express it well?
Does it make sense?
Does it matter?

Yes!

I must share myself
I must share my imagination
I must be heard
    If only by a few

The thoughts come in whispers
The thoughts come in shouts

Grab them
Put them to page
Write

annotation:

Like most people, my mood is affected by the weather.

Feeling Grey

gloomy

dreary

gray

dark

cold

sad

melancholy

that is how I describe today

a cold, grey, somber day

the sun left a week ago

it's done nothing but drizzle

       and rain for days on end

my mood matches the outside

downcast, sullen... lackluster

I have motivation, but not joy

I'm alert and awake, but ambivalent

I miss what little summer we had

I miss warm temperatures

I miss color outside

The leaves haven't even changed

What is there to look at, but

     gray, grey, and more gray?

sigh I miss happiness

I hope you enjoy this bonus content I call:

A Swirl of Emotions

The following 9 short stories are what inspired this book. They are based on a writing prompt I saw.

The goal was to write a complete story exactly 50 words long. I scoffed and thought it impossible, but the idea had already taken hold.

They are published in the order written with "Grief" being the story that sparked the ideas for the others.

Grief

He walks past the door. There's crying on the other side, but he doesn't pause to check on the occupant. He knows who's supposed to be in there. He also knows it's not possible. He buried his wife last week. And while he feels callous, he can't help her now.

Imagination

Flowers tickle her nose. A grin creases her face. Joy pours out of her as she lies in the grass. A cool breeze across her skin, ruffling her hair and clothes. Her mother shouts at her. Tells her to get up. "Brush the snow off your pants, first," she demands.

Boredom

It's the third sigh she's had in an hour. Her eyes glaze over. She has so much to do, but nothing holds her attention. The clock strikes 4:30. She smiles, gathers her things, and heads home. Alone on the couch, the tv flickers. She sighs again for the third time.

Excitement

Happy pants, joyful licks, and playful bounces. *She's home! She's home!* he cries internally. His tongue hangs and his eyes shine. He follows her from room to room. Finally, she turns and pets him. His heart fills to the brim. He runs and grabs his tennis ball. Time to play!

Devastation

He sits on the curb, his head in his hands. Tears are masked by heavy rain. He exhales. There's alcohol on his breath. Flashing lights strobe, but he barely registers them thru closed eyelids. His world is skewed, but the person in the other car... their world is irrevocably damaged.

Play Time

The kick of a ball, the crack of a bat, the slap of a jump rope on the blacktop. Children run around laughing, chasing, playing. An occasional tumble causes the masses to pause briefly. But after the tears dry, the grins and chattering begin anew. Recess is the best class.

Sleep

Beeping. An accidental alarm is going off. Groggy eyes open to see the time, and to find the snooze. Silence falls. Eyes close back up. Minutes pass. The alarm beeps again. With a groan of effort, the person sits up. They turn off the alarm and see the date. Saturday.

Depression

His life is filled with hobbies. He takes every class and joins all the groups he can. But none are his friends. He's busy, and appears happy, which he mostly is. But for all the human interaction he gets, he's lonely. His home is devoid of company. Sadness often encroaches.

The Process

Fifty words. That's not much space to write, yet so much can be said. Too many ideas swirl thru my head, but they disappear before I can put them to the page. I grab what I can and hope they're good. They show a myriad of emotions – the human experience.

About the author

Nicki Snyder currently lives in Wisconsin with her family, and a menagerie of pets.

And while she dislikes the cold, she loves the beauty of the area, and the warmth of the people that she's met there.

A Myriad of Emotions is Nicki's first book of poetry, but it won't be her last. She is currently working on a collection of quirky poems.

Nicki had been writing since she was a young teen, at the encouragement of her friends and teachers. Her first book, *The Circus Elephant*, was published when she was 19, and was written in middle school as a class project.

Reading, writing, and drawing have always been hobbies of the author, and now she is able to combine her loves into published works.

She hopes to never run out of creative ideas.

www.ingramcontent.com/pod-product-compliance
Lightning Source LLC
Chambersburg PA
CBHW051330120626

46547CB00016B/2483